BERLIN
THE CITY AT A GLANCE

C000113024

Unter den Linden

Berlin's famed promenade is n
its sticky lime trees. Highlights
Stalinist Russian Consulate and
Library, a below-ground memo
Nazi book-burning at Bebelplat

Gendarmenmarkt

This is the look of 18th-century Berlin,
Frederick the Great-style. The Konzerthaus is
home to the Berlin Symphony Orchestra and
it has a great winter market at Christmas.

Museum Island

A UNESCO world heritage site with five superb
museums. See the Ishtar Gate at the Pergamon
and the bust of Nefertiti in the Altes Museum.

TV Tower

This iconic landmark was built in the 1960s
by the GDR, who were irritated to find that
when the sun shines on their 'ball on a spike',
its reflection appears as a giant crucifix.
See p015

Checkpoint Charlie

The main border crossing between east
and west during the Cold War is now a rather
embarrassing tourist circus, and it's hard
to picture the tense stand-offs of the 1960s.

GSW Headquarters

Sauerbruch Hutton's renovation of a 1950s
office building is one of the most attractive
examples of urban renewal in the city.
See p013

Karl-Marx-Allee

Communism's version of the Champs-Elysées
has lousy shops, but the CSA Bar, Café Moskau
and Kino International are well worth a visit.
See p057

INTRODUCTION

THE CHANGING FACE OF THE URBAN SCENE

Berlin is now one of the world's great creative capitals, brimming with exhibitions and parties. What it lacks in fat cats and finance, when compared with Frankfurt or Munich, it makes up for with chutzpah and its own distinctive style. Cultural events such as Art Forum (www.art-forum-berlin.com), the Berlinale film festival (www.berlinale.de), Berlin Biennale (www.berlinbiennale) and Designmai (www.designmai.de) attract international attention, while fashion fairs like Premium (www.premiumexhibitions.com) put the city on the style map.

The standard and variety of eateries, shops and hotels have dramatically improved over the past few years to accommodate the discerning tastes of the many 'new Berliners' who flock to the city, whether they be Swiss, Brits or Swedes visiting for business, pleasure or politics. Members-only venues, such as China Club Berlin (Adlon-Palais, Behrenstraße 72, T 209 120), and restaurants with VIP rooms would have been unthinkable here five years ago, but are now thriving. In terms of nightlife, Berlin is full of contrasts: no one blinks an eye at film stars dancing at underground student parties or luxury automobile launches in derelict former factories. In fact, this is the attraction. Berlin is edgy but comparatively safe. It has a solid, tolerant municipal infrastructure, so that no matter how wild and late your partying, there's always a custard-coloured taxi on hand to whisk you back to your hotel.

ESSENTIAL INFO

FACTS, FIGURES AND USEFUL ADDRESSES

TOURIST OFFICE
Berlin Infostores
Brandenburger Tor, Hauptbahnhof
T 250 025
www.berlin-tourist-information.de

TRANSPORT
Car hire
Hertz
Tegel Airport
T 4170 4674
www.hertz.com
Europcar
Alexanderplatz 8
T 240 7900
www.europcar.com
Taxis
Funk Taxi Berlin
T 26 10 26
Trains
Deutsche Bahn
www.bahn.de

EMERGENCY SERVICES
Ambulance
T 112
Fire
T 112
Police
T 110
24-hour pharmacy
T 31 00 31

EMBASSIES
British Embassy
Wilhelmstraße 70-71
T 204 570
www.britbot.de
US Embassy
Neustädtische Kirchstraße 4-5
T 238 5174
www.berlin.usembassy.gov

MONEY
American Express
Bayreuther Straße 37-38
T 2147 6292
travel.americanexpress.com

POSTAL SERVICES
Post Office
Bahnhof Zoologischer Garten
Hardenbergplatz
T 018 023 333
Shipping
UPS
T 0800 882 6630
www.ups.com

BOOKS
Berlin Alexanderplatz by Alfred Döblin
(S Fischer Verlag)
Goodbye to Berlin by Christopher
Isherwood (Vintage)

WEBSITES
Architecture
www.archinform.net
Art/Design
www.artnews.info
Newspapers
service.spiegel.de/cache/international
www.berlinerzeitung.com

COST OF LIVING
Taxi from Tegel Airport to Mitte
£21
Cappuccino
£2
Packet of cigarettes
£3.20
Daily newspaper
£0.55
Bottle of champagne
£55

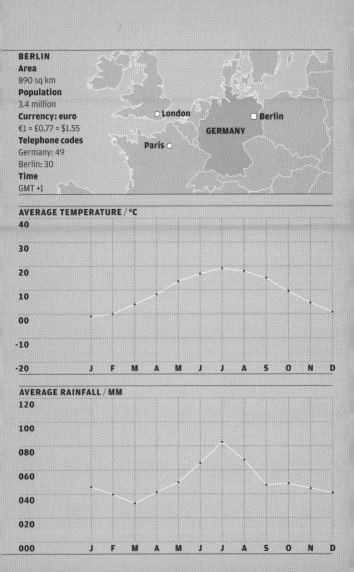

BERLIN
Area
890 sq km
Population
3.4 million
Currency: euro
€1 = £0.77 = $1.55
Telephone codes
Germany: 49
Berlin: 30
Time
GMT +1

London
Berlin
GERMANY
Paris

AVERAGE TEMPERATURE / °C

AVERAGE RAINFALL / MM

NEIGHBOURHOODS

THE AREAS YOU NEED TO KNOW AND WHY

To help you navigate the city, we've chosen the most interesting districts (see below and the map inside the back cover) and colour-coded our featured venues, according to their location; those venues that are outside these areas are not coloured.

TIERGARTEN

This huge park in the centre of Berlin is bisected by Straße des 17 Juni, which leads to the Brandenburg Gate. Apart from the Reichstag and Potsdamer Platz, modernist architectural gems by Oscar Niemeyer, Arne Jacobsen, Alvar Aalto and the like are to be found in the Hansaviertel.

KREUZBERG

Once the hangout of left-wing punks and anarchists, things have changed radically here since reunification, but the area has remained a healthy mix of cultures. In summer, it's a happy place to chill out, eat and socialise, especially around Schlesische Straße and Oranienstraße.

FRIEDRICHSHAIN

First impressions tend to be of huge six-lane roads lined with epic communist-era architecture, old stretches of Wall covered in bad paintings and large building plots. But dive off into the side streets around Simon-Dach-Straße and you'll find cafés, bars, retro furniture shops and restaurants.

CHARLOTTENBURG

There's no doubt that this district has suffered as a result of reunification, but Kurfürstendamm (or Ku'damm for short), the main shopping drag, is worth a look. And, recently, hip hotels such as Hotel Q! (see p030) have taken up residence here. Plus, the food halls of KaDeWe (T 21 210) department store are not to be missed.

MITTE

The historical city centre was the first area to be colonised by artists and gentrified after reunification. Today, it is a dramatic mix of refurbished 18th- and 19th-century apartment buildings, GDR *Plattenbauten* (prefabs) and contemporary architecture. The Scheunenviertel neighbourhood is touristy and full of international flagship stores, but the back streets are packed with interesting boutiques and restaurants.

PRENZLAUER BERG

Many of the 19th-century houses in this once decaying working-class district have been spruced up and are now occupied by arty types with small children. The scene currently centres around Knaackstraße or Kollwitzplatz. Lazy Sunday breakfasts in the cafés are de rigueur – if the kids don't don't drive you to distraction, that is.

SCHÖNEBERG AND WILMERSDORF

The leafy boroughs of the former west are home to grand old hotels, such as the Schlosshotel im Grunewald (see p024) and the Brandenburger Hof (see p017). From here, it's a short hop out to the lakefront area around the Wannsee (see p097) and the longest inland beach in Europe.

LANDMARKS

THE SHAPE OF THE CITY SKYLINE

The landmark most visitors want to see is the one that no longer exists: the Berlin Wall. Forget the appallingly tourist mock-up of the former Checkpoint Charlie near Friedrichstraße and head for the more poignant Berlin Wall Memorial on Bernauer Straße and Ackerstraße (www.berliner-mauer-dokumentationszentrum.de).

Just as the traces left by the Wall are increasingly hard to find, as the city expands into the gaps left by history, so are differences between 'east' and 'west'. The stretch of new internationalist and Stalinist architecture from Alexanderplatz down Karl-Marx-Allee is unmistakably 'east', but you'd be hard put to find any communist drab in the renovated area it leads to around Oberbaum City (see overleaf) and the bars on Simon-Dach-Straße in Friedrichshain.

Despite being two cities for 40 years, Berlin is so well labelled and has such an efficient and omnipresent public transport system of trains, buses, underground and trams that it's difficult to get lost. The only headache is the doubling up of buildings, like opera houses Deutsche Oper in the west (Bismarckstraße 35, T 343 8401) with Staatsoper in the east (Unter den Linden 7, T 2035 4438) and congress centres ICC (west, see p012) with BCC (east, see p065). Even confusion between the east and west stations of Ostbahnhof and Bahnhof Zoologischer Garten has now been resolved with the 2006 opening of the huge Hauptbahnhof (Europaplatz). *For full addresses, see Resources.*

ty

...old Narva electric lightbulb ...w been redeveloped into ...enovated Oberbaum City ...porary glass cube has been ...riginal brick Narva Tower, ...t up at night, is a 63m-high ...se heading east. The private ...n floor can be hired out for ...s stunning sunset views.

8-26

ICC (Internationales Congress Centrum)

A great, aluminium-clad, mothership of a monument to the times when the car was king in the eyes of the town planners, this 1970s congress centre by Ralf Schüler and Ursulina Schüler-Witte is now something of a dinosaur. It was state of the art when built with 80 halls that can host 20,000 people, electronic information boards and chairs with integrated headphones, reading lamps and desks. The eight-lane underground entrance can process 800 cars in 30 minutes and automated seating in the auditorium folds up against the walls to convert the space into a concert hall. It was the largest, most expensive building in Germany in its day, but with the advent of more modern multipurpose event halls, it looks like the ICC's days are numbered.

Neue Kantstraße/Messedamm,
T 3038 3000, www.icc-berlin.de

GSW Headquarters

This refit of a 1950s Kreuzberg high rise, with its clever façade of movable red metal scales and dishy curve, put local architects Sauerbruch Hutton well and truly on the map when the building was completed in 1999. The west-facing double-skinned exterior is covered with blinds in shades of red, orange and pink, which all open and close independently, both regulating the building's heat and light levels and making for a rather stunning piece of 21-storey abstract art. The structure is best appreciated in the golden glow of the evening sun from the lounge of the nearby panorama bar Solar (see p058). *Kochstraße 22*

Kaiser-Wilhelm-Gedächtnis-Kirche

This large and at first architecturally rather unremarkable church, designed by Franz Heinrich Schwechten in the 1890s, was severely bomb-damaged during the war. In the 1950s a debate raged about whether to tear the whole thing down or rebuild it. The final decision to have Berlin's great functionalist architect Egon Eiermann adapt the ruined torso of the tower into a memorial chapel and build a new church and bell tower to go with it was pioneering at the time. The stunning deep blue windows flecked with red and gold by Gabriel Loire in the interior of the octagonal church help create a suitably reflective atmosphere for what must surely be one of the most famous architectural monuments to the futility of war.
Breitscheidplatz, T 2147 6321,
www.gedaechtniskirche.com

TV Tower

Berlin's highest building, a distinctive 368m spike with a ball in the middle, is a valuable orientation point. Designed by an architects' collective and based on a 1960s concept by Hermann Henselmann and Jörg Streitparth, the Fernsehturm is a highlight of the new internationalist architecture around the Alexanderplatz area, much of which has now, sadly, been obscured, 'modernised' or torn down by unappreciative developers. The tower at least has remained and the former GDR symbol has since become a signature building for the unified city. The somewhat queasy express lift has now been replaced, so – if you can bear the queues – take the 40-second trip 207m up to the rotating Telecafé to drink in the panoramic views. *Panoramastraße 1a, T 242 3333, www.berlinerfernsehturm.de*

HOTELS

WHERE TO STAY AND WHICH ROOMS TO BOOK

There are more than 570 places to stay in Berlin and new hotels seem to sprout up overnight. Most of them are to be found in the former west, apart from those in Mitte, such as the splendid Hotel de Rome (Behrenstraße 37, T 460 6090). Staying east in any style is nigh on impossible, which is bizarre as Prenzlauer Berg and Friedrichshain are the up-and-coming residential areas.

Prices are extremely reasonable for a capital, so little wonder Berlin is one of Europe's top four city-break destinations. However, many new hotels are clones of international chains and finding a hideaway that combines great location, décor and service is more difficult. For shopping, dining and discretion in Mitte, Dorint Sofitel am Gendarmenmarkt (Charlottenstraße 50-52, T 203 750) and The Regent (Charlottenstraße 49, T 20 338) are ideal. If you are visiting during the Berlinale, a Potsdamer Platz address is a must – try the Grand Hyatt (see p027) and book well ahead. A great addition to Scheunenviertel, with its selection of designer boutiques, is the Lux 11 (see p018), an ideal base for Fashion Week. Otherwise, don't be afraid of tradition and 'go west' to one of the hostels off the Ku'damm, such as Pension Dittberner (see p028). Also check out hip boutique pads Hotel Q! (see p030) and Ku'damm 101 (Kurfürstendamm 101, T 520 0550), or wallow in the pompous splendour of Schlosshotel im Grunewald (see p024). *For full addresses and room rates, see Resources.*

Brandenburger Hof

A discreet and tranquil five-star oasis just a stone's throw from the Ku'damm, this hotel has been refurbished with a choice furniture selection, including Missoni rugs, Chanel lamps and Moroso chairs. The suites, such as the Demi (above) are not the biggest in town, but you stay here for the service and the details and not the acreage: Brandenburger Hof even has its own ikebana master, who places delightful flower arrangements in every room, while the concierge, Birgit Detrers, can conjure the impossible, such as last-minute tickets to the Philharmonie (see p038). There is a beautiful winter garden, surrounded by 'salons' perfect for private dinners, and the kitchen of the Die Quadriga restaurant (see p049) is superb.
Eislebener Straße 14, T 214 050,
www.brandenburger-hof.com

Lux 11

A much-needed recent addition to the Scheunenviertel district in Mitte, Lux 11 is a stylish boutique hotel housed in a former GDR banana warehouse and army officers' residence, and perfectly located for shopping and clubbing in the capital. The hotel's large, fully equipped junior suites (left) are ideal for longer stays and even the standard rooms come with surprisingly elegant kitchenettes. From the moment you enter reception (above), it's evident that the styling at Lux 11 is minimal – muted tones, smooth concrete and fur throws – but there is no skimping on quality and the beds are a joy. The service can be a little on the snooty side. *Rosa-Luxemburg-Straße 9-13, T 936 2800, www.lux11.de*

Askanischer Hof

One of the city's best kept secrets, the Askanischer Hof is the *Lieblingshotel* (favourite hotel) of many visiting actors, literary types and photographers. For spacious old Berlin townhouse style and spotlessly clean rooms at affordable prices, it is unparalleled in the city. The eclectic interior furnishings effortlessly span the gamut of 20th-century genres, with an élan that makes location scouts start to go weak at the knees. Rooms 15 (above) and 16 are particularly fine. *Kurfürstendamm 53, T 881 8033, www.askanischer-hof.de*

Hôtel Concorde

Designed by architect Jan Kleihues, this is one of the many new hotels in town and creates quite an impression with its 17 storeys of retro 1920s New York-style façade on a corner opposite the famous Café Kranzler (T 887 183 925). Rooms and suites are spacious and well decorated. The 10th and 11th Executive Floors have their own lounge space, where you can eat breakfast or dinner away from the throng staying in the 300-odd rooms. The best are the almost blindingly white Concorde Suite 904 and the semi-circular Concorde Suite 1002 (overleaf), with its panoramic bathroom.

Augsburger Straße 41, T 800 9990,
www.hotelconcordeberlin.com

Suite 1002, Hôtel Concorde

Grand Hyatt

Despite the pleasure-seeking, Potsdamer Platz-visiting tourist throng outside, the Hyatt is a classy hotel. The lobby (above) is all sleek wood and subdued colours, making it a welcome break from the usual country mansion look found in most five-star hotels. The rooms are both spacious and elegant with, thankfully, nary a floral print in sight. The Spanish architect José Rafael Moneo and Swiss designer Hannes Wettstein of Zürich's 9D Design have achieved a soothing environment of opulent minimalism in the top-floor Club Olympus Fitness Centre & Spa. The pool offers great views of the city. *Marlene-Dietrich-Platz 2, T 2553 1234, www.berlin.grand.hyatt.de*

Pension Dittberner

The main suite at the Dittberner, with its Marianne Koplin bedside lamps, raw silk chaise longue, stucco ceiling and splendid balcony overlooking a quiet street near the Ku'damm, is a lesson in classic west Berlin apartment living. This may only be a pension, but the elegance of the larger rooms beats the pants off most of the big-name hotels, at a fraction of the price. If you can't bear the thought of having no room service, you could always lodge the entourage in the other 21 rooms and send out for *Schwarzwälder Kirschtorte* (Black Forest gateau) from Harry Genenz (T 881 2537) on nearby Brandenburgische Straße. *Wielandstraße 26, T 884 6950, www.hotel-dittberner.de*

Hotel Q!
Following the success of the 'art hotel'
genre, a new crop of boutique hotels
is arriving on the scene and the Q! is all
curved corners, deep reds, dark wood
and slate, with a private members' bar
and a wellness centre with a hot sand
floor. The sexy Penthouse (pictured) is,
as you'd imagine, an aesthetic delight.
Knesebeckstraße 67, T 810 0660,
www.loock-hotels.com

24 HOURS
SEE THE BEST OF THE CITY IN JUST ONE DAY

Berlin is a 24-hour city and only your personal stamina can tell you when it's time to turn in. The working day begins at 8am and can end as early as 4pm, although new Mitte media types tend to go for the international, 10am until late, schedule. Weekends start at Friday lunchtime in summer as people head to country dachas or fill up the city's beer gardens and outdoor cafés. Promenading is a favourite pastime and locals and visitors alike throng to the latest architectural additions, municipal building open days or exhibitions on Museum Island. Barbecues in the park are also de rigueur, or nabbing a deckchair in a beach bar like Strandbar Mitte (Monbijoustraße 3, T 283 6877) along the Spree. If you fancy a stroll, the Soviet War Memorial in Treptower Park is worth a visit, as is the enormous weekend flea market on Straße des 17 Juni.

There is a breathtaking variety of nightlife, from concerts and clubs to impromptu open-air cinemas, parties and performances that are a Berlin speciality, often held in vacant lots and disused buildings. Pick up flyers or ask the locals. After you've partied until dawn, a favourite Berlin tonic is *currywurst* at Konnopke's Imbiss sausage stall (Schönhauser Allee 44a, T 422 7765) under the U-Bahn tracks. Opulent breakfasts are served all day in most cafés – try Nola's am Weinberg (Veteranenstraße 9, T 4404 0766) – so you can grab some well-earned sleep before starting all over again. *For full addresses, see Resources.*

08.00 Jogging beside the Spree

The towpath that follows the Spree river from Monbijoupark past Museum Island (Museumsinsel) to the Reichstag and the chain of government buildings near Marie-Elizabeth-Lüders-Haus is called the Spreebogen. It will take you about 30 minutes at a gentle trot and is a good chance to see all the new government architecture from its best angle. You can loop back on the other side of the river by crossing over the Santiago Calatrava-designed Kronprinzen Bridge or continue towards the Tiergarten if you're feeling fit.
www.museen-berlin.de

10.00 Café Einstein

After a quick freshen-up in the hotel you will now have well and truly earned your second breakfast. Berliners do *Frühstück* in style and the old Café Einstein (not to be confused with the branch at Unter den Linden 42, T 204 3632) is the perfect setting with a traditional feel. Try a glass of fresh orange juice, coffee and the Viennese breakfast, which includes fluffy rolls and two peeled soft-boiled eggs in

a glass. Add butter and season, gather the day's papers around you and enjoy. In the summer you can sit outside in the garden. *Kurfürstenstraße 58, T 261 5096, www.cafeeinstein.com*

12.00 Holocaust Memorial

Nestled between the Brandenburg Gate and Potsdamer Platz is the Memorial to the Murdered Jews of Europe, designed by Peter Eisenmann and unveiled in 2005. This impressive monument comprises an undulating field of 2,711 tightly packed stone monoliths that fills an entire block. You may wonder why it took Berlin so long to get around to building the monument, but with all the debate surrounding it – from the government rejecting the original designs and the row about whether it ought also to honour other Holocaust victims to the scandal of the contract for the graffiti-proof paint used on the stones being given to a firm whose sister company made the Zyklon B used in the gas chambers – it is a wonder that it ever got built at all. *Stresemannstraße 90, T 2639 4336, www.holocaust-mahnmal.de*

16.00 Neue Nationalgalerie

Walk west through Potsdamer Platz for 15 minutes and take in an exhibition — or just the building — at the Neue Nationalgalerie. Don't be surprised if Mies van der Rohe's masterpiece looks empty, as almost all the exhibition space is below ground. Mies' use of reflected light gives the impression that this massive structure is floating in space. *Potsdamer Straße 50, T 266 2651, www.neue-nationalgalerie.de*

20.00 Philharmonie

Tickets to a Philharmonie performance are a must if you can get hold of them; go for Brahms, Mahler or Bruckner, ideally conducted by Sir Simon Rattle if he is in town. The Philharmonic Hall is one of the world's most renowned concert spaces and is a masterpiece of expressionistic modernism. The architect, Hans Scharoun, was a product of the Bauhaus generation. His 1960s design was based upon the idea that the music should be at the centre and the 2,440 seats are arranged in a pattern of raked terraces all around the podium. The interior seems to spring into life during a performance as it fulfils its purpose: the unification of space, music and people. In this respect, it must be one of the most impressive public buildings in the world.
Herbert-von-Karajan-Straße 1, T 254 880, www.berliner-philharmoniker.de

22.30 Borchardt

The social status of being seated at one of the niche tables in Borchardt is not to be underestimated. The restaurant of choice for Berlin's celeb set is not only loved for its *plateaux de mer* and chilled Riesling but for the fine dramaturgy of its seating allocation. Tourists and potential stalkers are placed firmly front of house in this classic French-style brasserie of marble pillars and golden mosaics.

Borchardt also does a lovely *wiener schnitzel* and a delicious Kobe beef steak while asparagus is a regional speciality when in season.
Französische Straße 47, T 8188 6262

URBAN LIFE

CAFÉS, RESTAURANTS, BARS AND NIGHTCLUBS

The innumerable illegal clubs in hard-to-find, crumbly ruins with little ventilation and few fire exits that sprang up in the 1990s are fading into legend. Gentrification and the German compulsion to make everything neat and tidy has brought a new phase to Berlin. The city around Mitte has smartened up its image and hip bar and restaurant interiors have moved to the opposite extreme, with white upholstery and clinically clean lines currently in vogue.

Since MTV and Universal Music moved their HQs to riverside locations in the east, Friedrichshain and the part of Kreuzberg just over the Spree have become the new docklands. Clubs, restaurants and bars, such as Watergate Club (see p060) and Spindler & Klatt (see p050), as well as loft developments, are booming, but there is still enough of a rough, abandoned edge to keep it interesting. Or you could just grab a bottle or two of Tannenzäpfle beer, squeeze through a gap in the fence onto a derelict lot by the river and join one of the impromptu parties that dot the area in summer.

The west, particularly around the Ku'damm and Kantstraße, tends to have a rather staid image, but there are some signs of a renaissance in the form of the members' bar at Hotel Q! (see p030) and our old favourite, Universum Lounge (see p059). The grander establishments like the Paris Bar (see p053) and Café Einstein (see p034) are to be found here too and are still well worth a look. *For full addresses, see Resources.*

Shiro i Shiro

This recent addition to Berlin's restaurant culture is as much about seeing and being seen as the Asian fusion food (the name means 'white castle' in Japanese). The owner is Duc Ngo The, famed in the city for his elegant and reasonably priced Kuchi Japanese restaurants (www.kuchi.de). Dishes like lobster with pork belly and salsify with caramelised soy sauce are choreographed by young French-trained chefs in an open 'show kitchen' and the décor was designed by Korean Hyun Jung Kim and Vietnamese-born Truong Ngu, who did the Kuchi interiors. A highlight is the 50-seat banqueting table inlaid with mother of pearl (above).

Rosa-Luxemburg-Straße 11, T 9700 4790, www.shiroishiro.com

Newton Bar
Named after the late Helmut Newton
and his life-sized photographs of naked
amazons in high heels on the wall,
this classic bar has a gentlemen's club
feel with its updated art deco interior of
polished-wood panelling and stuffed
leather armchairs by Hans Kolhoff. The
upstairs cigar lounge is great for parties.
*Charlottenstraße 56, T 2029 5421,
www.newton-bar.de*

Schneeweiß

Until recently, the Simon-Dach-Straße area in Friedrichshain was the preserve of backpackers, students and the odd pioneer, but now the restaurant density has reached interesting proportions. The most attractive new addition is the lovely Schneeweiß, with its snow-white interior designed by Unit Berlin. The 'alpine' menu is more Austrian foothills than peak cuisine, with tasty dishes such as *Kaiserschmarrn* (sugared pancake with raisins) and *Flammkuchen* (onion tart), but prices are pretty reasonable and here the atmosphere is everything.
*Simplonstraße 16, T 2904 9704,
www.schneeweiss-berlin.de*

Susuru

The latest street to be colonised by the Scheunenviertel boutique expansion is also home to a fresh new udon noodle bar. Susuru (meaning 'slurping' in Japanese) is Berlin-based interior designer Romann Fehrentz's dream project. Inspired by the cult Japanese film *Tampopo* (directed by Juzo Itami), he designed the whole interior down to the tiniest detail and opened with the modest ambition of becoming the best

damn noodle place in town – and he's not far off. It is an ideal midday stop-off with a seasonal menu and lovely thick noodles with just the right amount of bite, all at very reasonable prices.
Rosa-Luxemburg-Straße 17, T 211 1182, www.susuru.de

Vau

If you're in the mood for power-dining in a stern, masculine interior, this is where you should come. Maître de cuisine Kolja Kleeberg was awarded a Michelin star within a year of opening Vau and the pearwood-panelled interior and vaulted ceilings were designed by the architect Meinhard von Gerkan (who also created the new Hauptbahnhof and Olympiastadion redevelopment, see p093). The seasonal menu is a sophisticated, grown-up take on local classics like *maultaschen* (German ravioli) and *schupfnudeln* (potato noodles), along with fascinating combinations like cold Jerusalem artichoke soup with quail egg yolks and a side of venison tartare. *Jägerstraße 54-55, T 202 9730, www.vau-berlin.de*

White Trash Fast Food

This cult location originally occupied an old Chinese restaurant venue in nearby Torstraße, complete with plastic dragon wall decorations and little lanterns. Now it has taken over the dark-wood interior of a former traditional-style Irish pub and plastered every inch of wall with kitsch paraphernalia. The ethos seems to be: if it stays still long enough, decorate it, which might explain the in-house tattoo parlour and barbershop. A haven for English-speaking alternative creatives, who come for the quirky DJs, rock/punk/country/trash bands and, of course, the fast food, this is typical Berlin when you are in the mood for a bit of lowlife (open from 6pm). *Schönhauser Allee 6-7, T 5034 8668, www.whitetrashfastfood.com*

Die Quadriga

When the master chef Bobby Bräuer took over the kitchen here, he was soon being hailed as one of the top three chefs in town. He calls his cuisine 'quintessential' and tends to concentrate on seasonal and regional ingredients, such as venison and chestnuts from the Bavarian village of Polting or Pauillac lamb and lavender from Provence. Die Quadriga somewhat bravely serves only German wines with its food, but with a superb cellar of more than 850 bottles and a 2003 Gault Millau Wine List of the Year distinction, there is no better place to be pleasantly surprised by what *les Allemands* are capable of in world-class viniculture as well as cuisine. *Eislebener Straße 14, T 214 050, www.brandenburger-hof.com*

Spindler & Klatt
This Zen lounge-style club/restaurant
venue is in a former warehouse with
a terrace on the riverfront. Inside is the
complete lounging, dining, cocktails and
dancing experience; you could happily
stay here all night. For dinner, the Black
Angus rib-eye steak and enormous king
prawns atop salad are recommended.
*Köpenicker Straße 16-17, T 6956 6775,
www.spindlerklatt.com*

Bangaluu

Mitte's new restaurant and cocktail bar is just the ticket for clean freaks on a night out: white carpets, upholstery, curtains and walls reflect the current penchant for snowy hues. Bite-sized 10-course set menus are served from 9pm sharp, with dainty portions to avoid the danger of soup on the suit, and there's a smoking ban in the restaurant too. The theme is not new: a blend of lounge, dance and reclining dining – think the Supperclub in Amsterdam meets Nektar in Munich with décor *à la* Hillside Su Hotel in Antalya and you'll have the mix – but it's tastefully done, notably the VIP restaurant upstairs. *Invalidenstraße 30, T 809 693 077, www.bangaluu.com*

Paris Bar

This classic French brasserie-style bar and restaurant near the Theater des Westens (T 31 90 30) is a second home for a regular crowd of actors, artists and celebrities who seem to have been here forever. The walls are lined with art by the late Martin Kippenberger, who was a friend of the owner Michel Würthle, and whose work (as does the bar) epitomises Berlin in the 1980s, although the venue actually opened in the 1960s and has been packed ever since. The food and drinks are fine but not spectacular, but you should come here for the crowd, not the cuisine. *Kantstraße 152, T 313 8052*

40 Seconds

There is a trend towards panorama bars in Berlin and this club gets its name from the 40-second journey up in the lift. The 360-degree view of Potsdamer Platz is splendid from the three terraces, and with three lounges, a bar and a (winter) restaurant, there's plenty of space to shake a leg. Saturday's best for clubbing.
Potsdamer Straße 58, T 8906 4241, www.40seconds.de

KMA 36

Situated next to the classic Café Moskau (T 2463 1626) in an international style glass pavilion that used to be a cosmetics studio in GDR times, this is the perfect place to start your weekend club tour, rubbing shoulders with other discerning night owls. The décor is neither kitsch nor 'ostalgic', as is often the case with other bars that play on their eastern heritage, although it can vary according to what exhibition is on show or which launch party has just been hosted. The martini cocktails and whisky sours are memorable, which is why it's standing room only after 10pm.
Karl-Marx-Allee 36

CSA Bar

It's become an oft-cited classic over the last few years but is still not to be beaten. This delightfully elegant little bar in the former offices of the Czech Republic's airline CSA (hence the name: pronounced Ché-Ess-Ah Bar) used to be an oasis in the desert until Friedrichshain really took off as a desirable neighbourhood. The plump leather seating and attention to interior details, superb cocktails, lovely ambience,

good music, discreet staff and exotic location within the Stalinist architecture of this famous street all contribute to make this an essential Berlin watering hole.
Karl-Marx-Allee 96, T 2904 4741

Solar

Our favourite view of the city is from this
15th-floor restaurant and club. Enter the
anonymous high rise near the ruins of
Anhalter Bahnhof, once one of Berlin's
largest stations that was destroyed in
WWII, take the vertigo-inducing glass
lift up the side of the building to the
restaurant and climb the spiral staircase
to the well-appointed bar. Then gradually
slip into the next day sipping sekt or an
apero on ice while attempting to point out
the city landmarks you've memorised
from your Wallpaper* City Guide.
*Stresemannstraße 76, T 16 3765 2700,
www.solarberlin.com*

Universum Lounge

Voted Wallpaper's Best Bar in 2003, Universum is still a big favourite, with its lounge take on the Houston Apollo Project designed by interior wizards Plajer & Franz (see p062). Situated on the ground floor of the lovely 1926 cinema designed by Erich Mendelsohn, which now houses the Schaubühne theatre, the chunky brass front of the bar complements the white leather upholstery, while brass chain curtains keep out the real world. With cocktail lists stowed in slots in the teak tables ready for take-off, the digital wall clock showing Houston time and some early space-travel cibachromes to get you in the mood, after a few shots of rocket fuel you'll be crooning *Fly Me to the Moon* into the wee hours.
Kurfürstendamm 153, T 8906 4995, www.universumlounge.com

Watergate Club
It's more of a club than a bar, but it's also a great place to relax over an evening Watermelon Man cocktail. Either sip it on the floating waterfront terrace or looking out from the two-storey glass façade with views of the grand dockland warehouse architecture and Oberbaum Bridge with its Disney-esque turrets.
Falckensteinstraße 49, T 6128 0396, www.water-gate.de

INSIDERS' GUIDE

ALEXANDER PLAJER & WERNER FRANZ, INTERIOR DESIGNERS

Indefatigable interior designer duo Alexander Plajer and Werner Franz are familiar figures on the Berlin party circuit. They also designed top watering holes Universum Lounge (see p059) and Bar Lounge 808 (Oranienburger Straße 42-43, T 2804 6727), as well as the various Caras coffee houses and Brille 54 shops around town. For Plajer and Franz there is no typical Berlin nosh, 'apart from barbaric *Eisbein* (ham shank) or *Currywurst* (curried sausage)', but there are plenty of creative foreign delicacies.

In the mornings they recommend a Portuguese coffee and pastry at the lovely Café Galão (Weinbergsweg 8, T 4404 6882) or an *integrale* breakfast at the café and bar 103 (Kastanienallee 49, T 4849 2651). For lunch on the hoof, a döner kebab somewhere on the Kottbusser Tor: 'We prefer the hottest sauce and cool it down with a glass of *ayran* (a Turkish yogurt drink).'

For a special evening meal, their favourite restaurant is Facil (Potsdamer Straße 3, T 590 051 234), 'a stylish place with fantastic food and even better service'. But, they say, you can easily blow your entire budget there in one night. A great alternative is Solar (see p058), which has 'a fantastic view', or that other top vantage point and currently one of the hippest clubs in town, Weekend (Am Alexanderplatz 5, www.week-end-berlin.de), on the 12th floor of a GDR prefab looking out over Alexanderplatz.

For full addresses, see Resources.

ARCHITOUR

A GUIDE TO BERLIN'S ICONIC BUILDINGS

You can't beat Berlin for its panoply of 20th-century architecture, from Bauhaus via new internationalist to new brutalist, with all the shades of ugly, charming and ridiculous in between. Its many architectural showpieces include Hans Scharoun's golden concert hall the Philharmonie (see p038), Daniel Libeskind's quirky Jewish Museum (see p066), Norman Foster's revamped Reichstag (Platz der Republik 1), the fabulous TV Tower (see p015) and Mies van der Rohe's iconic Neue Nationalgalerie (see p036). In fact, Berlin has so many gems, from Peter Behrens' 1909 AEG Turbine Hall (Huttenstraße 12-19) to Foster's Philological Library (Habelschwerdter Allee 45), that we can only list the highlights.

Despite all the new buildings, it is still fascinating to compare GDR and FRG architecture trends, such as the grandiose Stalinist street Karl-Marx-Allee, which leads on to Hermann Henselmann's slightly later internationalist building group near Alexanderplatz, including the Haus des Lehrers (opposite), Haus des Reisens (Alexanderplatz 5), Café Moskau (Karl-Marx-Allee 34, T 2463 1626) and Kino International cinema (Karl-Marx-Allee 33, T 2475 6011). The west Berlin equivalent is the slightly less bombastic but still impressive structures of the 1957 International Builders' Exhibition (Interbau) in Hansaviertel in the Tiergarten, with examples by Oscar Niemeyer, Walter Gropius and Werner Düttmann.

For full addresses, see Resources.

BCC and Haus des Lehrers

This fabulous building ensemble by the GDR architect Hermann Henselmann, who is responsible for much of the new international style in east Berlin, has been lovingly restored. The complex comprises the 1964 low-slung, dome-roofed Berlin Congress Centre (BCC) and neighbouring Haus des Lehrers, 'teachers' house' (Alexanderplatz 3), which is wrapped in a stunning two-storey façade mosaic by Walter Womacka. The congress hall has a wealth of architectural details, including a sculptural metal frieze running around the circular interior walls. Original details and sympathetic modernisation make this one of our favourite structures in Berlin.
Alexanderstraße 11, T 2380 6750,
www.bcc-berlin.de

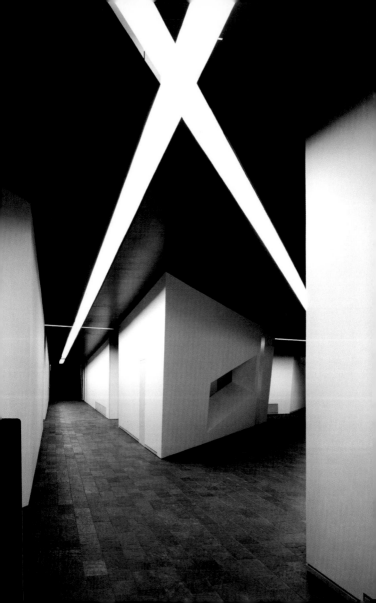

Jewish Museum

You either love it or you hate it. Daniel Libeskind's museum caused a sensation in 1999, but it doesn't seem to be ageing very well. The uncompromising intensity of the architecture – a titanium-zinc skin lasered through with oblique, cleft-like openings and voids and acutely angled interiors – looked fabulously sculptural when it was empty, but now seems rather at odds with the exhibition it was built to house. Nevertheless, it makes a striking and impressive statement, and the little maze-like Garden of Exile is one of the most memorable and ingenious garden concepts you are likely to see anywhere. *Lindenstraße 9-14, T 2599 3300, www.juedisches-museum-berlin.de*

DZ Bank

Restrained by strict building regulations in this historically sensitive location on Pariser Platz between the Hotel Adlon Kempinski and the Brandenburg Gate, Frank Gehry's first building in Berlin, the former DG Bank, which was finished in 1999, saves deconstructivist surprises for the interior. The deceptively plain limestone façade gives way to a writhing fish-like form (a common inspiration for Gehry) in glass, wood and metal that dominates the central atrium. The shiny, curvaceous belly of the 'whale' houses a function room and an auditorium for this office and residential block. Jonah must be turning in his grave.
Pariser Platz 3

Le Corbusier Haus

Initially, Le Corbusier's bold contribution to Berlin's cityscape was meant to rub shoulders with architectural gems by Oscar Niemeyer and Arne Jacobsen in the Tiergarten as part of 1957's Interbau exhibition. But once Le Corbusier stated his intention to build a 17-storey, 557-unit 'residential factory', city authorities found him a more suitable location. And so this classic *unité d'habitation*, built in 1958, finished up as a misplaced *wohnmaschine* for 1,400 residents on top of a hill next to the Olympiastadion (see p093). Most of the shops are long gone, but the building is popular with young architect first-time buyers keen to experience both modular living and spectacular city views. *Flatowallee 16*

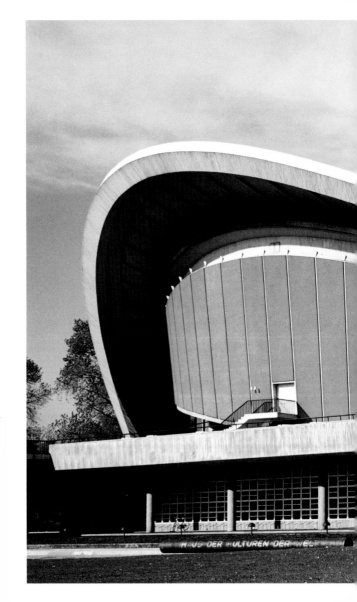

Haus der Kulturen der Welt
This former congress centre, built by the
American architect Hugh Stubbins in 1957,
is currently undergoing a refit. Thanks
to the shape of its huge, concrete-shell
roof, it's known as the 'pregnant oyster'
(locals love to nickname their buildings).
The shallow pool out front is home
to a Henry Moore bronze, *Big Butterfly*.
*John-Foster-Dulles-Allee 10, T 397 870,
www.hkw.de*

SHOPPING

THE BEST RETAIL THERAPY AND WHAT TO BUY

Shopping in Berlin is an eclectic experience. If you want big labels, stick to KaDeWe (Tauentzienstraße 21-24, T 21 210) and Ku'damm, where you will find Bulgari, Tiffany, Gucci, Chanel and Prada, although Friedrichstraße, with its Galeries Lafayette (76-78, T 209 480) and Quartier 206 (71, T 2094 6240), is becoming a more select option. The Mitte shopping area, centred around Neue and Alte Schönhauser Straße, has now expanded down many little side streets and into Rosa-Luxemburg-Straße near Alexanderplatz. Here you'll find boutiques, handmade wallpaper and lovely lingerie shops jostling for space between roadworks, glaziers and bridalwear hires. Keep in mind that some places may take a bit of hunting and an adventurous spirit to seek out. F95 (see p077), for example, brings a whiff of Colette way out east to Friedrichshain and Andreas Murkudis' huddle of ultramodern shops (AM1, AM2 and AM3, see p086) is hidden at the back of a crumbling courtyard in Mitte – even locals struggle to find them.

If you're looking to stock up on more specialised items that are distinctly 'Berlin', then high-quality kitchen accessories from WMF at KaDeWe or a Bauhaus dinner service from KPM (Unter den Linden 35, T 206 4150) are good bets. Or perhaps let your hair down with something more frivolous, such as bespoke headwear from Fiona Bennett (Große Hamburger Straße 25, T 2809 6330). *For full addresses, see Resources.*

Bless

Fashion's answer to Droog, this design collective turns out inspiring and unique clothing, jewellery and accessories, many of which have a conceptual bent, such as the 'Cable' jewellery (above, starting from €80). You can also buy wooden storage boxes for your clothes that are shaped like sweaters and dresses. The interior of the store is forever changing and if you would like to take the whole experience home with you, you can purchase Bless wallscapes – mural-size photographic panels of places were Bless products have been sold. Since many of them include shelves to store your gear on, you get the feeling of walking into a collage.
Mulackstraße 38, T 2759 6566,
www.bless-service.de

Hugo

Though the German super-label Hugo Boss is generally known for its relatively restrained interpretation of current trends, this prototype concept shop takes the prize for Mitte OTT. The brainchild of in-house creative director Volker Kächele, the Hugo store occupies an early 1900s building and comes complete with acres of mirrors, a 1:500 scale, 3D relief of the Mitte district arranged on the walls, and an 8m-tall bamboo forest in the courtyard. The clothes and accessories, on the other hand, are reassuringly Hugo, in other words sleek, chic and reasonably priced.
Rosenthaler Straße 49, T 2888 4550, www.hugoboss.de

F95

Think Colette meets Berlin's wild, wild east and you've got the idea of F95. The organisers of the Berlin Premium fashion fair offer 400 sq m of up-and-coming labels, accessories and cosmetics, all of which have bucketloads of promise. Shop for jeans by Earnest Sewn, leather bags by Pauric Sweeney, silver skull-and-bones necklaces by Corpus Christi or scents by Miller Harris. If you're in a more cultural mood, flip through CDs from Blue Flame Records or peruse the book selection, which ranges from Riefenstahl's photos of Africa to Rizzoli's Tom Ford tome.
Frankfurter Allee 95-97, T 4208 3358, www.f95store.com

Blush Dessous

This is the place to find delicious lingerie from owner Claudia Kleinert's own label, as well as a hand-picked selection of silky skimpies from the likes of Fifi Chachnil, Cavalli and Malizia in saucy, purple-tinted boudoir surroundings. The store's pièce de résistance is a king-sized, brown velvet-upholstered 1970s bed, complete with retro radio in the headboard. Shopping companions can be left to lounge here with a selection of cult German magazines while you occupy yourself with the serious business of what not to wear.
Rosa-Luxemburg-Straße 22, T 2809 3580, www.blush-berlin.com

The Corner Berlin

A temple to good taste on the corner of the elegant Gendarmenmarkt square in Mitte, The Corner Berlin is owned by Josef R Voelk, former manager of the nearby Quartier 206 (T 2094 6240). Its cool white and brown interior, designed by Gonzales Haase, houses an exquisite selection of must-haves, including men's and women's fashion from Balenciaga and Veronique Branquino, cosmetics by Ren, vintage Eames furniture and arty books from Assouline. If all that shopping gets your stomach rumbling, refuel at the in-store bar and restaurant, Eat at The Corner. *Französische Straße 40, T 2067 0940, www.thecornerberlin.de*

Pro qm

Tucked away in a side street in the hip
Scheunenviertel, this is a must visit
for print medium fetishists. Run by
Jesko Fezer, Katja Reichard and Axel
Wieder, Pro qm (meaning 'per sq m')
offers a superb selection of German
lifestyle mags and books on design,
graphics, architecture and pop culture.
*Almstadtstraße 48-50, T 2472 8520,
www.pro-qm.de*

Stue

'Useful 20th-century objects from Denmark' says the sign in the window. Essential is more like it. Every couple of weeks or so, owners Elke Penzlien and Heike Maria Rädeker tootle off to Denmark (and occasionally Sweden and Finland) in their van and come back laden with furnishing treasures, including vintage ceramics, teak tables, light fixtures and earth-toned sofas and chairs. If trying to carry a coffee table through customs sounds daunting (though it clearly doesn't bother the owners), then shipping purchases home is an option. *Torstraße 70, T 2472 7850*

Erich Hamann Bittere Schokoladen

This is a rare thing in Berlin: a shop that has survived two world wars, the post-war renovation obsession and the division of the city. Erich Hamann started making chocolate in 1912. As his confectionery was located around the corner from a girls' boarding school, his takings soon boomed. Today, his great-grandson runs the business. The lovely art deco chrome and satinwood fittings of the shop have not changed since 1928, and the delicious dark bitter chocolate is so exquisite that you'll want to buy whole suitcases full of it.
Brandenburgische Straße 17, T 873 2085

Über

This concept shop's themed installations
change every three months or so,
like those of the surrounding galleries in
Auguststraße, so there are always new
and irresistibly quirky household items
to discover. A recent theme of *Leichtigkeit*
(lightness), for example, included pieces
of jewellery made out of feathers, a
trampoline and a salad dryer in the form
of a light cloth bag. The reason behind
the frequent changes, says owner Anja
Kantowsky, is that she loves 'the hunt for
the unusual' and to bring 'movement and
sensuality to the everyday'. A permanent
feature at Über, on the other hand, are the
gorgeous George Nelson 'Bubble Lamps',
which were originally intended as lighting
for the shop but proved so popular that
Kantowsky now stocks the whole range.
An ingenious and totally delightful store.
Auguststraße 26a, T 6677 9095,
www.ueber-store.de

AM1, AM2 and AM3

The only drawback of Andreas Murkudis' trio of delightful shops is their hidden location. But once you've tracked them down, you can happily shop for vintage-style Schiesser underwear, Johnston's cashmere, Yohji Yamamoto, Haltbar, Martin Margiela and Andreas' brother's label, Kostas Murkudis, as well as pieces by select local designers. AM's good taste even extends to stocking Erich Hamann

chocolate (see p083). The cutting-edge interiors of the shops were designed by the Berlin-based Gonzales Haase Architects. *Münzstraße 21-23, T 3088 1945*

Herr von Eden

The Herr sells suits and accessories that span seven decades. The emphasis was originally on vintage finds, but now that supplies of original 1930s and 1940s suits are running low, you can also choose from owner Bent Jensen's retro-inspired in-house label. Herr von Eden's selection ranges from Harris and Norfolk tweeds to bankers' pinstripes and collegiate grey flannels. The store also stocks shirts and neckties, plus masculine-style women's jackets, trousers and shirts.
Alte Schönhauser Straße 14, T 2404 8682, www.herrvoneden.com

SPORTS AND SPAS

WORK OUT, CHILL OUT OR JUST WATCH

Being flat, Berlin is a haven for cycling, and an extensive network of paths makes this one of the best ways to get around town. In the summer, Deutsche Bahn leaves distinctive hire bikes dotted around the city (www.callabike.de), which you can pick up and ride, using your mobile phone to pay (T 0700 0522 5522).

Still basking in the warm afterglow of the World Cup, the Olympiastadion (see p093), built for the 1936 Olympics, is an impressive venue, and if you are a football fan it is worth getting tickets to see the local team, Hertha BSC (www.herthabsc.de).

The city has a high proportion of public swimming pools per capita, some of which are the most beautiful and well equipped in Europe. But opening times are at best erratic and at worst plain annoying. Ask your concierge to undertake the complex detective work. Alternatively, the well-kept lakes surrounding the city offer bathing and sailing in the summer or ice skating in the winter.

Berlin is only slowly waking up to the pleasures of pampering, and spas are mainly restricted to hotels and Holmes Place (Am Gendarmenmarkt, Friedrichstraße 68, T 2062 4949), going under the heading of 'Wellness' areas. The Yi Spa (see p092) is a fine addition to Mitte, otherwise check out the Club Olympus Spa & Fitness in the Grand Hyatt (see p027) or Ku'damm 101 (Ku'damm 101, T 520 0550) and Hotel Q! (see p030) in Charlottenburg. *For full addresses, see Resources.*

Landsberger Allee Swimming Complex

Originally proposed as part of Berlin's bid to host the 2000 Olympic Games, the Senat decided to console itself over losing out to Sydney by going ahead and building the largest swimming complex in Europe anyway. There's no doubt that French architect Dominique Perrault has created a building of great beauty and technical quality, which, with its adjoining velodrome (overleaf), nestles almost totally underground below shimmering metal roofs and a huge apple orchard. The glass, beechwood, steel and white-tiled interior is flooded with light and harmonises well with the deep blue of the four main pools. It provides training facilities that any serious international swimmer would give their webbed toes for, and the diving tower even has its own lift.
Paul-Heyse-Straße 26, T 4218 6120

Landsberger Allee Velodrome

Yi Spa

This spa calls itself a stress reduction and revitalisation oasis. The interior has the usual Zen-inspired feel, but the cosy, dark chocolate brown and grey colour scheme with hot pink highlights makes it warm and welcoming. The staff are well versed in a range of delightful massages, from Hawaiian to deep tissue sports massage and their own version of hot stone therapy. Body wraps and scrubs, as well as facials using enticing ingredients, such as coconut, chocolate, bananas and mango and honey, are also on offer, plus a superb foot massage. *Monbijouplatz 3a, T 2887 9665, www.yi-spa.com*

Olympiastadion

This iconic oval by Werner March may owe its external form to its National Socialist past, but inside it is a superb example of contemporary stadium design. Originally built to house the infamous 1936 Summer Olympics, it was renovated between 2000 and 2004 by Hamburg architects Gerkan, Marg and Partner (Gmp) in preparation for hosting the 2006 World Cup Final. The limestone façade is deceptive; the inside is scooped out and more than half of the stadium is below ground. Gmp lowered the pitch by a further 2.65m to increase the seating capacity to 74,200, and added a delicate, translucent roof membrane which slots seamlessly into the original structure. *Olympischer Platz 3, T 3068 8100, www.olympiastadion-berlin.de*

Badeschiff

What started off as an urban regeneration experiment to enliven the neglected river area has now turned into one of Berlin's favourite R&R venues. The Badeschiff ('bathing ship') is essentially an old river barge floating on the Spree that has been cleverly refitted as a heated pool by AMP in collaboration with local architect Gil Wilk and artist Susanne Lorenz. The wood decking and docklands ambience, plus regular events and DJs, make it a perfect post-industrial venue for a lazy afternoon. In the winter, cocoon-like coverings keep the heated pool, bar, sauna and massage area cosy and warm in a rather bizarre and stunning contrast to the ice floe-filled river. *Eichenstraße 4, T 553 2030, www.badeschiff.de*

ESCAPES

WHERE TO GO IF YOU WANT TO LEAVE TOWN

It's not easy to run out of things to do in Berlin, but if you do find yourself needing some respite from partying, you can take a train to just about anywhere in Europe from the new Hauptbahnhof (Europaplatz, www.bahn.de). With Poland less than 100km away, heading east is a good option. Closer to Berlin are Hamburg (one hour via the high-speed link); Dresden (two hours), the former baroque capital of Europe; and Leipzig (just over an hour).

If you prefer to get back to nature, there is a myriad of sandy-shored lakes on the city outskirts and in surrounding Brandenburg. On a warm summer's day, the Werbellinsee, about an hour's drive north, is particularly lovely, while in winter, packing a hot toddy and spending the day ice skating on the lakes is heavenly.

Potsdam, the former summer residence of the Hohenzollerns, was trashed by WWII and East German road traffic planners, but is now a well-restored pretty baroque town on Berlin's outskirts that has become a tourist magnet. Crowds visiting the Sanssouci palace and gardens can be a drag in summer, but a pilgrimage to Erich Mendelsohn's fabulously expressionist Einstein Tower (see p100) is well worth the walk through the Albert Einstein Science Park. A rare piece of contemporary architecture hidden behind a baroque façade in the town centre is Rudy Ricciotti's snow-white interior of the Nikolaisaal Concert Hall (see p101).

For full addresses, see Resources.

Wannsee Strandbad

If you have a hankering for messing about in a boat, but don't have time for a long trip, you don't have to leave the city. The Wannsee is a sprawling lake complex surrounded by forest that is part of the city's second main river, the Havel. It's southwest of Berlin just before Potsdam, about 20 minutes by train. Wannsee Strandbad is one of the longest inland beaches in Europe, where you can hire rowing boats and lounge in the distinctive wicker chairs. To avoid the crowds, sailing is much more relaxing but you'll need to befriend a local with a yacht or talk to your concierge: hotel Brandenburger Hof (see p017), for example, offers a day trip in a vintage motor launch along with a guide and gourmet hamper.

GFZK Gallery, Leipzig
The Saxony city of Leipzig has a cultural
tradition of art, book fairs, education
and JS Bach, and the politically minded
GFZK Gallery mounts exhibits and funds
projects that aim to examine the role of
art in a post-socialist country. Not that
the gallery is rejecting capitalism in
any way – its café and bar are thriving.
Karl-Tauchnitz-Straße 11, Leipzig
T 0341 140 810, www.gfzk.de

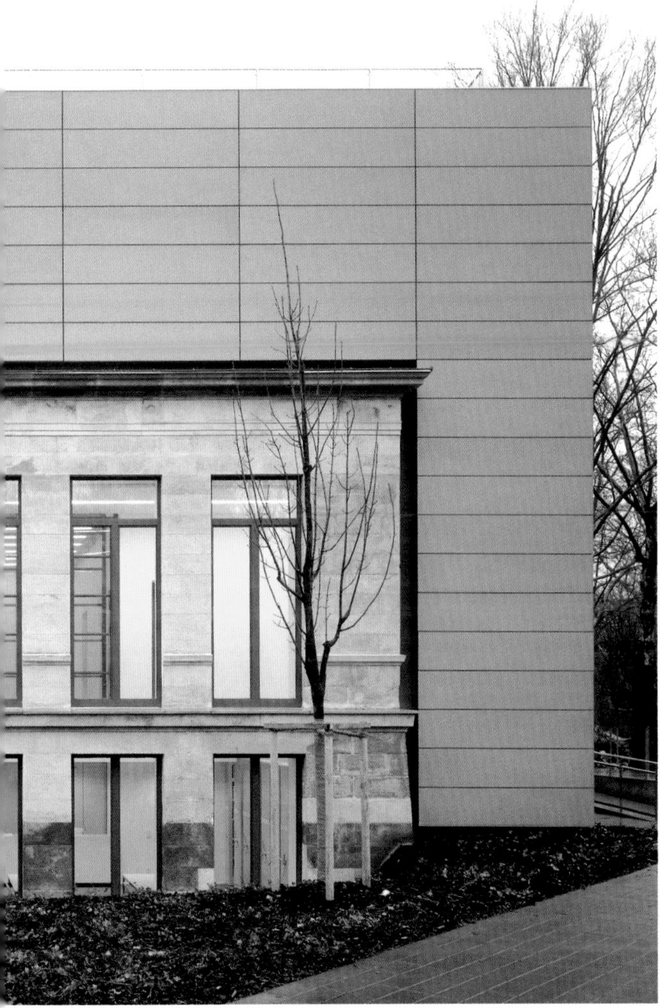

Einstein Tower, Potsdam

This curious tower was designed in 1920 by Erich Mendelsohn for the astronomer Erwin Finlay-Freundlich to observe the sun and work to substantiate Einstein's Theory of Relativity. The building was so experimental that it only remains in place thanks to constant renovation work, as the early concrete from which it was constructed is just not up to the structural tasks required of it. Legend has it that Mendelsohn took Einstein on a tour of the tower to get his impression. Einstein's one-word review: 'organic'. Visit before the law of entropy finally gets the upper hand.

Telegrafenberg, Potsdam

Nikolaisaal Concert Hall, Potsdam

This former community hall in a courtyard near the Nikolai church fell into disrepair after the war and was given to the city by the parish in 1981. The French architect Rudy Ricciotti was later commissioned to convert it into a modern 750-seat concert hall and it opened its doors in 2000. The wavy surface of the interior (overleaf), somewhat deconstructivist with ironic art deco references, makes for a surprising contrast to the façade and ticket office (above) and a warm, saturated acoustic. The rather provincial music programme is somewhat disappointing, though: a mixed bag including Ludwig van Beethoven, Jan Garbarek concerts and celebrity evenings. *Wilhelm-Staab-Straße 10-11, Potsdam T 0331 288 8828, www.nikolaisaal.de*

Nikolaisaal Concert Hall

NOTES
SKETCHES AND MEMOS

RESOURCES
CITY GUIDE DIRECTORY

A

AEG Turbine Hall 064
Huttenstraße 12-19

AM1, AM2 and AM3 086
Münzstraße 21-23
T 3088 1945

B

Badeschiff 094
Eichenstraße 4
T 553 2030
www.badeschiff.de

Bar Lounge 808 062
Oranienburger Straße 42-43
T 2804 6727

BCC 065
Alexanderstraße 11
T 2380 6750
www.bcc-berlin.de

Bless 073
Mulackstraße 38
T 2759 6566
www.bless-service.de

Blush Dessous 078
Rosa-Luxemburg-Straße 22
T 2809 3580
www.blush-berlin.com

Borchardt 039
Französische Straße 47
T 8188 6262

Bangaluu 052
Invalidenstraße 30
T 809 693 077
www.bangaluu.com

C

Café Einstein 034
Kurfürstenstraße 58
T 261 5096
Unter den Linden 42
T 204 3632
www.cafeeinstein.com

Café Galão 062
Weinbergsweg 8
T 4404 6882
www.galao-berlin.de

Café Kranzler 021
Kurfürstendamm 18
T 887 183 925
www.cafekranzler.de

Café Moskau 056
Karl-Marx-Allee 34
T 2463 1626
www.das-moskau.com

China Club Berlin 003
Adlon-Palais
Behrenstraße 72
T 209 120
www.china-club-berlin.de

Club Olympus Spa & Fitness 088
Grand Hyatt
Marlene-Dietrich-Platz 2
T 2553 1234
www.berlin.hyatt.com

The Corner Berlin 079
Am Gendarmenmarkt
Französische Straße 40
T 2067 0940
www.thecornerberlin.de

CSA Bar 057
Karl-Marx-Allee 96
T 2904 4741

HOTELS
ADDRESSES AND ROOM RATES

Askanischer Hof 020
Room rates:
double, €130;
Room 15, €130;
Room 16, €132
Kurfürstendamm 53
T 881 8033
www.askanischer-hof.de

Brandenburger Hof 017
Room rates:
double, €245-€285;
Demi Suite, €350
Eislebener Straße 14
T 214 050
www.brandenburger-hof.com

**Dorint Sofitel
am Gendarmenmarkt** 016
Room rates:
double, €270
Charlottenstraße 50-52
T 203 750
www.dorint.de

Grand Hyatt 027
Room rates:
double, €240-€370
Marlene-Dietrich-Platz 2
T 2553 1234
www.berlin.grand.hyatt.de

Hôtel Concorde 021
Room rates:
double, from €230;
Concorde Suite 904
and 1002, €1055
Augsburger Straße 41
T 800 9990
www.hotelconcordeberlin.com

Hotel Q! 030
Room rates:
double, €170;
Penthouse, €330
Knesebeckstraße 67
T 810 0660
www.loock-hotels.com

Hotel de Rome 016
Room rates:
double, €520
Behrenstraße 37
T 460 6090
www.hotelderome.com

Ku'Damm 101 016
Room rates:
double, €98
Kurfürstendamm 101
T 520 0550
www.kudamm101.com

Lux 11 018
Room rates:
double, €125;
standard room, €125;
junior suite, €145
Rosa-Luxemburg-Straße 9-13
T 936 2800
www.lux11.de

The Regent 016
Room rates:
double, €310
Charlottenstraße 49
T 20 338
www.theregentberlin.com

Pension Dittberner 028
Room rates:
double, €110-€122;
suite, €133
Wielandstraße 26
T 884 6950
www.hotel-dittberner.de

Savoy 026
Room rates:
double, €230
Fasanenstraße 9-10
T 311 030
www.hotel-savoy.com

Schlosshotel im Grunewald 024
Room rates:
double, €255-€325;
Kaiser Suite, €2,500
Brahmsstraße 10
T 895 840
www.schlosshotelberlin.com

WALLPAPER* CITY GUIDES

Editorial Director
Richard Cook

Art Director
Loran Stosskopf

City Editor
Sophie Lovell

Project Editor
Rachael Moloney

Executive Managing Editor
Jessica Firmin

Chief Designer
Ben Blossom

Designer
Ingvild Sandal

Map Illustrator
Russell Bell

Photography Editor
Christopher Lands

Photography Assistant
Jasmine Labeau

Chief Sub-Editor
Jeremy Case

Sub-Editor
Nancy MacDonell

Assistant Sub-Editor
Milly Nolan

Wallpaper* Group
Editor-in-Chief
Tony Chambers

Publishing Director
Gord Ray

Publisher
Neil Sumner

Contributors
Paul Barnes
Jeroen Bergmans
Alan Fletcher
Sara Henrichs
David McKendrick
Claudia Perin
Meirion Pritchard
James Reid

Wallpaper* ® is a registered trademark of IPC Media Limited

All prices are correct at time of going to press, but are subject to change.

PHAIDON

Phaidon Press Limited
Regent's Wharf
All Saints Street
London N1 9PA

Phaidon Press Inc
180 Varick Street
New York, NY 10014

Phaidon® is a registered trademark of Phaidon Press Limited

www.phaidon.com

First published 2007
Reprinted 2008
© 2007 IPC Media Limited

ISBN 978 0 7148 4718 4

A CIP Catalogue record for this book is available from the British Library.

Printed in China

PHOTOGRAPHERS

Bitter Bredt
GSW Headquarters, p013
Jewish Museum,
pp066-067

Diephotodesigner.de
Berlin city view, inside
front cover
Lux 11, pp018-019
Askanischer Hof, p020
Pension Dittberner,
pp028-029
Spreebogen, p033
Café Einstein, p034
Holocaust Memorial, p035
Neue Nationalgalerie,
pp036-037
Borchardt, p039
Shiro i Shiro, p041
Susuru, p045
Vau, pp046-047
White Trash Fast
Food, p048
Die Quadriga, p049
Spindler & Klatt,
pp050-051
Bungalow Dinnerclub,
p052
Paris Bar, p053
40 Seconds, pp054-055
KMA 36, p056
CSA Bar, p057
Solar, p058
Alexander Plajer and
Werner Franz, p063

DZ Bank, p068
Le Corbusier Haus, p069
Bless, pp074-075
Hugo, p076
F95, p077
Pro Qm, pp080-081
Erich Hamann Bittere
Schokoladen, p083
AM1, AM2 and AM3, p086
Yi Spa, p092

Georges Fessy
Landsberger Allee
Swimming Complex,
p089, pp090-091

Heiner Leiska/Artur
Olympiastadion, p093

**Heinz Krimmer/
Voller Ernst**
Haus der Kulturen
der Welt, pp070-071

Noshe
ICC, p012

Reinhard Friedrich
Kaiser-Wilhelm-
Gedächtnis-Kirche, p014

Roland Halbe/Artur
Einstein Tower, p100

Patrick Voight
TV Tower, p015
Newton Bar, pp042-043
Schneeweiß, p044
Universum Lounge, p059
BCC and Haus des Lehrers,
p065

Philippe Rualt
Nikolaisaal, p101,
pp102-103

Sabine Götz
Wannsee Strandbad, p097

BERLIN
A COLOUR-CODED GUIDE TO THE HOT 'HOODS

TIERGARTEN
Berlin's central park is bordered by the Reichstag and the Potsdamer Platz

KREUZBERG
The cultural melting pot of the city with plenty of places to eat and socialise

FRIEDRICHSHAIN
Here you'll find avenues of communist architecture and side streets full of surprises

CHARLOTTENBURG
Home to the main shopping drag plus a host of upmarket restaurants and hotels

MITTE
The old city centre, exciting new architecture and stylish boutiques – it's all here

PRENZLAUER BERG
Known for its pretty 19th-century apartment buildings and Sunday brunches

SCHÖNEBERG AND WILMERSDORF
The leafy boulevards and grand villas of the old west lead out to the Wannsee lakes

For a full description of each neighbourhood, see the Introduction.
Featured venues are colour-coded, according to the district in which they are located.